The Life Cycle of Tarantulas

New Forest Press

NEWARK PUBLIC LIBRARY
121 HIGH ST.
NEWARK, NY 14513

An Hachette Company

First published in the United States by
New Forest Press, an imprint of Octopus Publishing Group Ltd

www.octopusbook.usa.com

Copyright © Octopus Publishing Group Ltd 2012

Published by arrangement with Black Rabbit Books
PO Box 784, Mankato, MN 56002

All rights reserved. No part of this work may be reproduced or utilized in any form or by any means, electronic or mechanical, including photocopying, recording or by any information storage and retrieval system, without the prior written permission of the publisher.

Library of Congress Cataloging-in-Publication Data

Twist, Clint.
The Life Cycle of Tarantulas / By Clint Twist.
p. cm. -- (Creepy Crawlies)
Includes index.
Summary: "Describes the life of a tarantula by explaining its body parts, habitat, and behaviors. Compares tarantulas to other spiders, shows how they spin webs and catch food. Includes life-cycle diagram and close-up photos of body parts"--Provided by publisher.
ISBN 978-1-84898-521-6 (hardcover, library bound)
1. Tarantulas--Life cycles--Juvenile literature. I. Title.
QL458.42.T5T848 2013
595.4'4--dc23
2012003599

Printed and bound in the USA

16 15 14 13 12 1 2 3 4 5

Publisher: Tim Cook   Editor: Margaret Parrish   Designer: Steve West

Picture credits:
b=bottom; c=center; t=top; r=right; l=left
Alamy: 8 (Danita Delimont), 15t (David Haynes), 17b (Jonathan Plant). Getty Images: 6-7 (Digital Vision). FLPA: 2-3 (Mark Jones/Minden Pictures), 4-5 (Michael & Patricia Fogden/Minden Pictures), 5 side panel, 9t, 12, 18, 19 side panel, 24b (Mark Moffett/Minden Pictures), 7t (Chris Mattison), 22 (Claus Meyer/Minden Pictures). OSF: 5, 13b (Nick Gordon), 21 side panel, 27t (Densey Clyne Productions). Science Photo Library: 9 side panel, 13 side panel (Steve Gschmeissner), 11 side panel, 17 side panel, (Sinclair Stammers), 15 side panel (Scott Camazine), 23 side panel (Andrew Syred).

Every effort has been made to trace the copyright holders, and we apologize in advance for any unintentional omissions. We would be pleased to insert the appropriate acknowledgments in any subsequent edition of this publication.

Contents

What are Tarantulas? 4
Up Close and Personal 6
Home, Snug Home 8
Trip Lines 10
Prowling for Prey 12
Spider Senses 14
Massive Jaws 16
Search for a Mate 18
Spiderlings 20
Tarantulas and Humans 22
Other Spiders 24
Spider Behavior 26
Life Cycle and Fabulous Facts 28
Glossary 30
Index 32

What are tarantulas?

Tarantulas are spiders. Spiders are wingless, eight-legged creatures. They are not insects, because insects have six legs and spiders have eight. Tarantulas are the largest of all spiders. Their legs can span 12 in (30 cm).

Tarantulas are predators. They are carnivores (meat-eaters) that hunt and kill other animals. Tarantulas eat mainly insects, but sometimes they hunt prey as big as birds!

The huge red-kneed tarantula shown here is found in Costa Rica.

Spiders live everywhere except the North and South poles and on mountaintops. These places are too cold. Tarantulas like warm regions like deserts and rainforests.

In the Know

Spiders are arachnids. Other kinds of arachnid are scorpions, ticks, and mites. Arachnids and insects are part of a larger group called arthropods. Adult arthropods do not have an inner skeleton made of bones like we do. Instead, they have a tough outer shell called an exoskeleton.

Tarantulas prefer hot, tropical regions like this one in Venezuela.

Spiders shed their exoskeletons as they grow.

Up Close and Personal

A large tarantula has a body that is about 2 in (5 cm) across. Most tarantulas are covered in lots of prickly hairs.

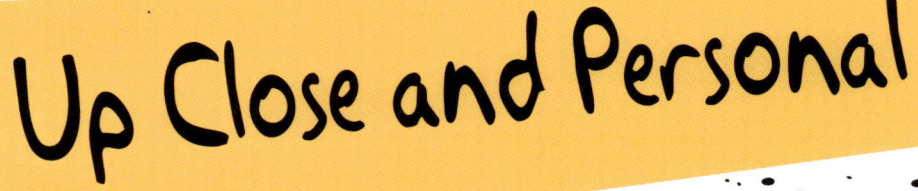

Legs

Fangs

Pedipalps

All spiders have two parts to their bodies: the prosoma and the abdomen. The front part of the prosoma is the spider's head and contains eyes, brain, strong jaws, and sharp fangs.

A pair of short pedipalps (arms) are used to hold food while the spider eats it. Four pairs of walking legs are behind the pedipalps.

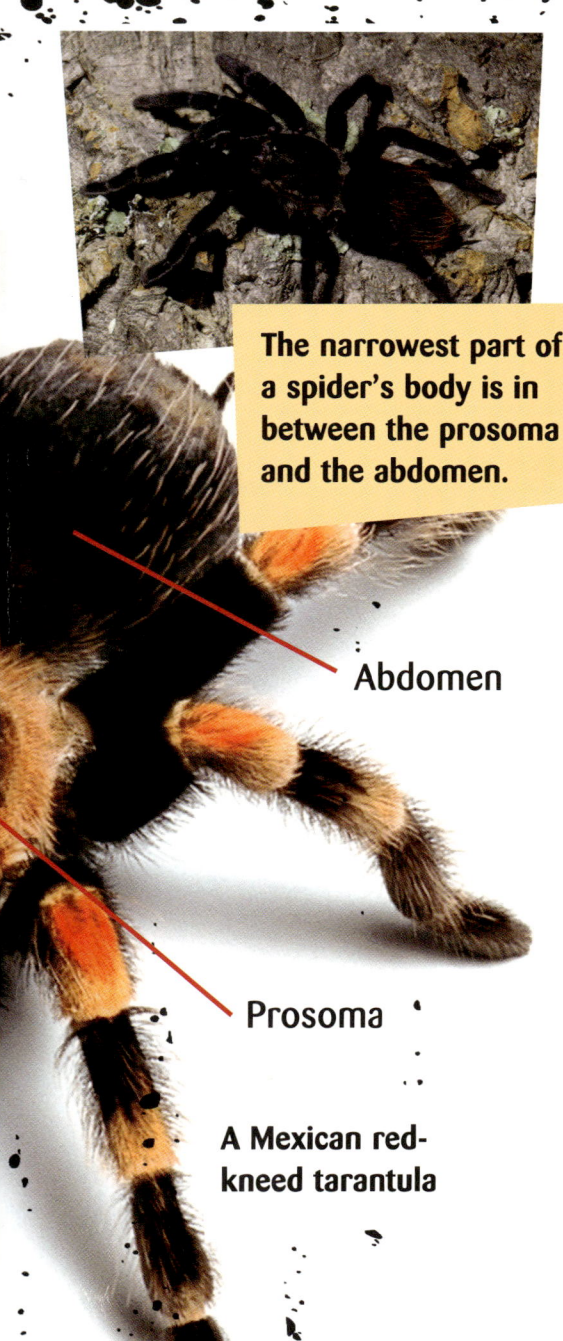

The narrowest part of a spider's body is in between the prosoma and the abdomen.

Abdomen

Prosoma

A Mexican red-kneed tarantula

Spider Shape

The earliest spiders probably had three body parts, like insects: head, thorax, and abdomen. With spiders, the head and thorax gradually joined to form a single part, called the prosoma.

A Brazilian pink tarantula

Special parts inside the abdomen produce silk. Tarantulas use silk to catch their prey and line their nests.

Home, Snug Home

Tarantulas live alone and do not form family groups. They can live a long time: females can live for up to 35 years, while males live to about half that age.

A tarantula likes a safe, dry, permanent nest, where it lives its whole adult life. Some live in holes in trees, but most prefer underground nests.

Strong jaws allow the tarantula to cut through even the hardest, sun-baked soil. Burrows can be 30 in (75 cm) deep.

The opening of the burrow is kept small, so other creatures can't enter. There is usually just one place in the burrow wide enough for the tarantula to turn around in.

This metallic pink-toe tarantula has spun a silk lining to make a cozy burrow.

Silk Production

Insects and spiders both produce silk. With insects, it is the larvae (young) that produce silk. With spiders, it is the adults. Some use silk to build webs; others to make trip lines or nests linings.

A tarantula's prey wrapped in silk

Trip Lines

Most tarantulas spend life hiding in burrows waiting for prey. After a big meal, the spider may not eat for several weeks.

Some spiders spin webs to catch flying insects or to trap those crawling on the ground, but not tarantulas. They don't spin webs, but do use silk to snare prey.

Tarantulas attack and kill prey with their sharp fangs, just like this raft spider is doing.

A tarantula spins trip lines that spread out from its burrow like spokes on a wheel. Hiding in its nest, the spider feels when its prey touches a line, and it pounces.

Paralyzing Poison

All spiders produce venom, which is made by glands in the head and injected through fangs in the jaws. Venom paralyzes a victim so that it cannot move while the spider eats it alive.

The tarantula settles down in its nest to wait for an unsuspecting vicitm.

An Antilles pink-toe tarantula

All tarantulas are meat-eaters. This one is feeding on a grasshopper.

11

Prowling for Prey

Some tarantulas are too impatient to wait for prey, so they go on the hunt. These include the largest bird-eating tarantulas.

It can be dangerous for tanantulas to leave the nest during the day. Their large size makes them tempting targets for spider-eating birds that spot them. Nighttime is safer, although there's still a chance the predator may become the prey.

This goliath bird-eating tarantula is feasting on a snake.

Liquid Steel

Spider silk starts out as a liquid squirted from spinnerets located in the spider's abdomen. The strands of silk harden but remain sticky. Spider silk is stronger than steel wire of the same thickness.

Tarantulas eat mostly insects. The biggest tarantulas attack small mammals, lizards, and even baby birds that they steal from nests!

If a tarantula cannot find large prey, it will collect lots of small insects. It then wraps them together in silk and eats them all at once.

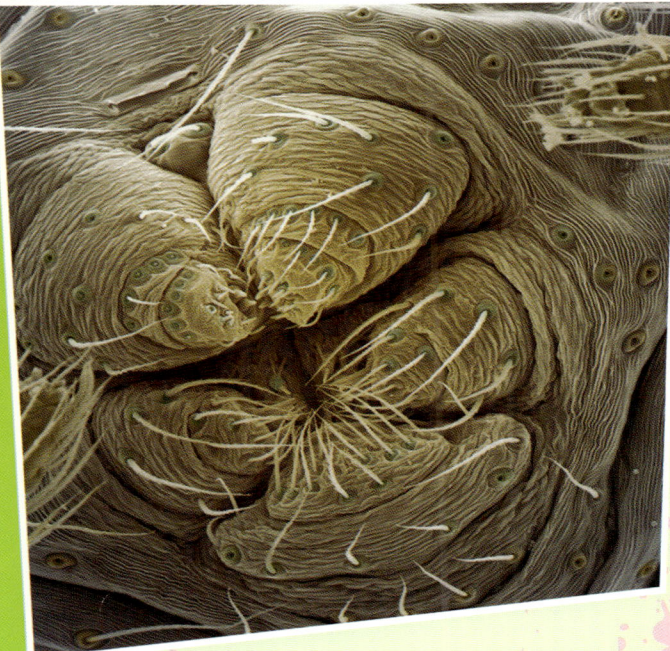

A tarantula's spinnerets

Spider Senses

Some spiders have excellent eyesight; others, including tarantulas, have very bad eyesight. All spiders, however, can feel vibrations, and this is how they find their way around.

Tarantulas can feel tiny vibrations through their legs and sense the direction of the movement.

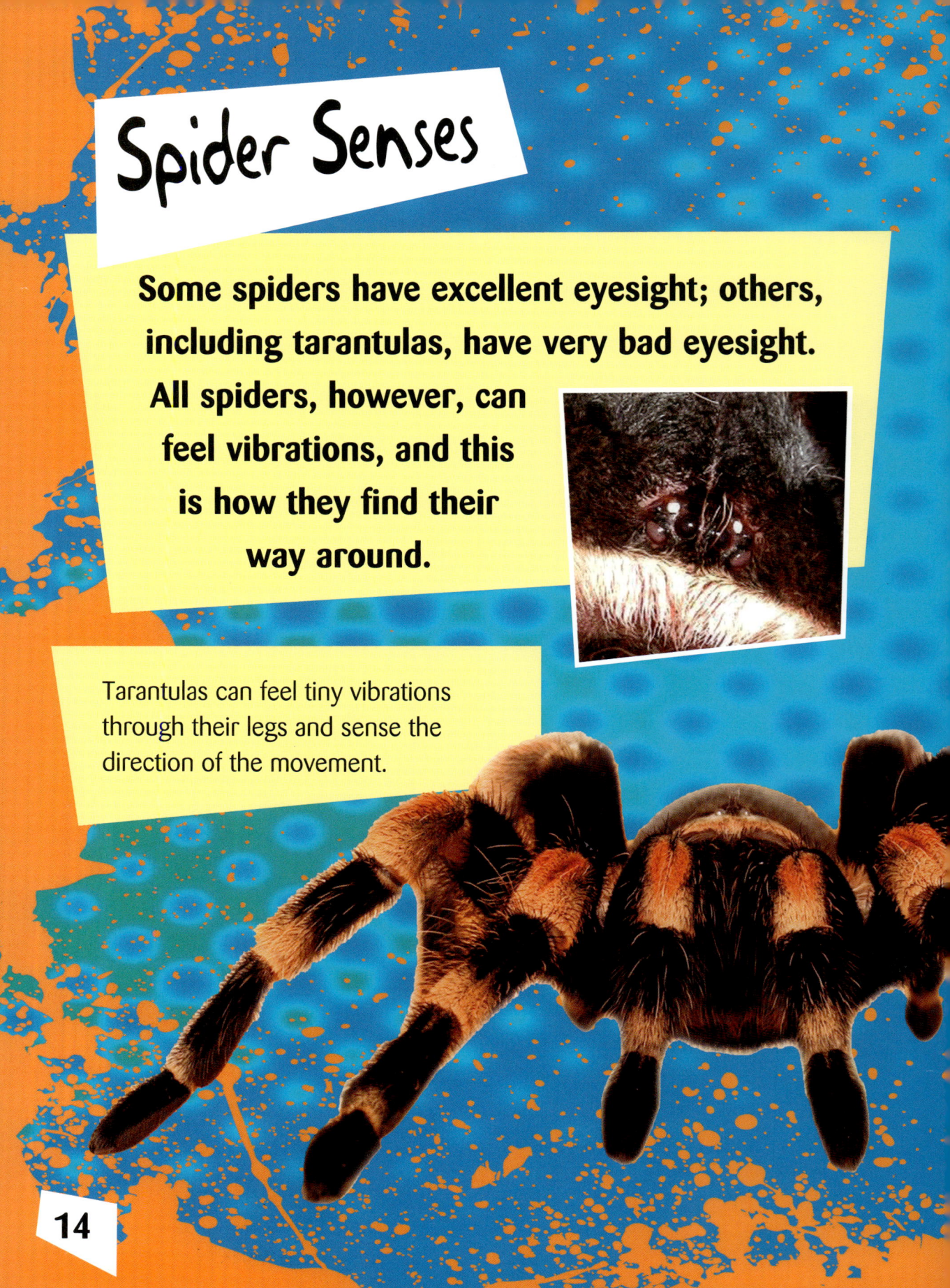

All spiders have hairs that pick up vibrations—even spiders that do not look hairy.

Tarantulas have eight small eyes at the front of the prosoma. Each eye can tell the difference between light and dark—just enough so the spider can detect movement.

A red-kneed tarantula from Mexico

Paired Eyes

Most spiders have eight eyes. Some have six or four, and some just two. Usually the eyes are arranged in two rows. Jumping spiders have two hunting eyes that can produce clear images, but most spiders have to make do with bad eyesight.

Spiders' eyes come in pairs. This jumping spider has four eyes.

Massive Jaws

Spiders are grouped by how their jaws work. Tarantulas belong to the first group, which has jaws that strike downward.

A tarantula's fangs are on the front of its prosoma.

Fangs

Tarantulas have two sharp fangs. They bite with both at once or with one after the other. Either way, their victim is killed.

Pincer fangs

Liquefied Food

Spiders do not chew their food—they slurp it. Once the prey stops moving, the spider dribbles digestive juices into it. The juices turn the prey's insides into a liquidy goo that the spider sucks into its mouth. After the meal, all that is left of the prey are some tiny pieces the spider can't eat.

The second group of spider has insward-striking jaws. The fangs come together like pincers and stop the prey from escaping.

This crab spider is sinking its fangs into a honey bee.

Fangs. The fangs of the Chile rose tarantula can pierce even the toughest insect exoskeleton.

Search for a Mate

Tarantulas develop slowly and are not able to mate until they are 10 years old. Mating takes place during the hottest and driest part of the year.

Males and females live separately, but they do not use special communication to find each other. Instead, finding a mate is a matter of chance.

A female California tarantula is alerted to a male outside her nest by her trip lines.

This Brazilian salmon bird-eating tarantula is defending itself.

Mating can be a risky business for males, because female tarantulas often prefer eating to mating—and they are quite happy to eat male tarantulas. Successful mating doesn't always mean safety for the male. After mating, the female may still have him as a tasty snack!

The male lifts the female up to mate, just as this Pampas gold tarantula is doing.

Safety Sound

Spiders make sounds and communicate by rubbing their legs together or drumming them on the ground. Males in search of a mate make a special safety sound when moving. The sound makes it less likely that the female will attack.

This jumping spider is making sure it is safe to mate with the female.

Spiderlings

Female tarantulas lay up to 1,000 eggs at once. The female holds the tiny eggs together with strands of silk in what is called an egg sac.

The egg sac is about half the size of the female's body. She leaves it in the deepest part of her burrow and doesn't care for it. If the burrow floods, however, she will carry the egg sac to safety.

A female wolf spider carries her egg sac.

The eggs hatch into tiny spiderlings that look like little adults, except that they are almost colorless. They feed on creatures in the soil that are too small to fill up an adult tarantula.

Spider Development

A spider's exoskeleton will not stretch as the spider grows. Instead, a growing spiderling develops a new, larger exoskeleton beneath the old one. When the new exoskeleton is ready, the old one splits open and is discarded. This process is called molting.

Pet tarantulas can be born and raised in captivity.

Tarantulas molt several times before they are grown.

Tarantulas and Humans

The spiders that we call tarantulas, even the biggest bird-eating ones, are not really dangerous to humans. Their powerful jaws can deliver a painful bite, but their venom is too weak to hurt us.

The name tarantula originally belonged to a much smaller, more dangerous spider. This original tarantula is the European wolf spider (Lycosa tarentula). The wolf spider was named tarantula after the town of Taranto in Southern Italy, where it is found.

The name Tarantula has now been given to the big hairy spiders, such as this bird-eating tarantula.

The European wolf spider was the original tarantula.

Scientists long ago discovered that even though the wolf spider delivers a painful bite, it does not pass diseases to humans.

Irritating Hairs

Tarantulas have other weapons besides fangs and venom. Their hairs are coated with poison and have sharp, fragile tips that break off easily. The poison on the hairs is not strong enough to harm a person, but if the tips become stuck in skin they can cause a painful rash.

Wolf spiders like this one are not as dangerous as people once thought.

Prickly hairs

Other Spiders

There are more than 40,000 species of spider. All have two body segments and eight legs—but that's where the similarities end.

Jumping spiders
One of the largest of the spider groups, jumping spiders have excellent eyesight and two pairs of eyes. They can spring up to 10 in (25 cm) to catch prey.

Curved spiny spider

Some spiders have spines and horns that give them an usual appearance. Scientists think the horns and spines are protection, making it difficult for birds to swallow them.

Flower spiders

Their funny sideways walk gives these spiders their second name—crab spiders. They have pale bodies and wait on flowers to catch visiting insects. Some change color to match the background flower.

Black widow

It is easy to recognize the famous black widow spider, thanks to its red marking. The bite of a black widow is very painful, and the poisonous venom is strong enough to kill children and the elderly.

Spider Behavior

Many spiders live and hunt in much the same way as tarantulas, but others have different ways of life—and very different ways of using their silk.

Web spinners
The most well-known spiders are those that spin webs between branches to catch flying insects. The spider sits at one corner of the web and waits for vibrations made by an insect tangled in the web.

Net-throwing spiders

These spiders do not make one fixed web. Instead, they spin a small web like a piece of fishing net. The spider holds the net between its front legs and waits patiently. When an insect comes within reach, the spider nets its victim.

Water spider

This spider is only found in fresh water. It spins a dense web of silk and then traps bubbles of air in the web. The air in the bubbles allows the spider to breathe under water while it waits for prey such as tadpoles and tiny fish.

Spitting spider

Spitting spiders have special venom-silk glands that allow them to spit two streams of poisonous silk. They attack their insect prey and cover their victims with a zigzag pattern of threads so they cannot escape.

Find Out More

Life Cycle

After mating with a male, the female produces an egg sac that can contain up to 1,000 tiny eggs. The egg sac is made of silk. Tiny spiderlings hatch from the eggs and emerge from the nest after a few weeks and have to find their own food. They grow into adults that will then find a mate and make more eggs.

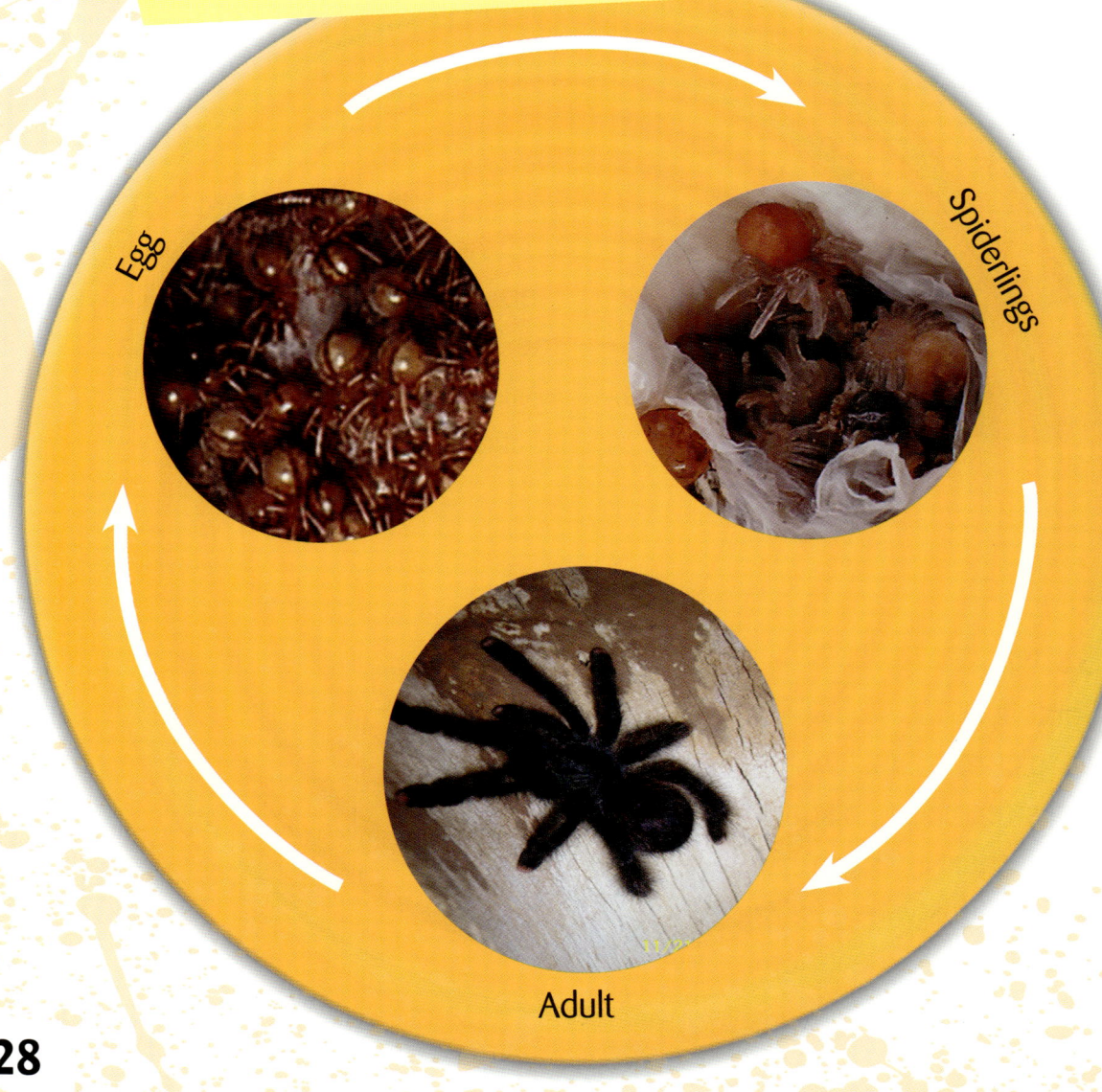

Egg

Spiderlings

Adult

Fabulous Facts

Fact 1: Tarantulas can be as small as a fingernail or as big as a dinner plate.

Fact 2: For most people, a tarantula bite is no worse than a bee sting.

Fact 3: Tarantulas have retractable claws, just like cats!

Fact 4: A tarantula spiderling will molt about 10 times before it becomes an adult.

Fact 5: Fear of spiders is called Arachnophobia. It is one of the most common fears among humans.

Fact 6: Some tarantulas eat lizards, birds, and even mice.

Fact 7: Tarantulas can be kept as house pets in a terrarium.

Fact 8: On average, female tarantulas live 20 to 30 years and males live 10 to 12 years.

Fact 9: Tarantulas do not make webs to catch their prey. Instead, they hide and rush out to attack prey when it comes along.

Fact 10: There are more than 800 species of tarantula.

Fact 11: When feeling threatened, some tarantulas make a loud hissing noise by rubbing the bristles on their legs together.

Fact 12: Some large animals and birds eat tarantulas. Some tarantula species are cannibalistic—they eat each other!.

Fact 13: Tarantulas like to live alone and will attack other tarantulas that come near them uninvited.

Glossary

Abdomen—the largest part of a spider's body; the abdomen contains many important organs.

Arachnids—a group of creepy crawlies that includes spiders, scorpions, ticks, and mites.

Arachnophobia—the fear of spiders.

Arthropod—any creepy crawly that has jointed legs; insects and spiders are arthropods.

Cannibal—an animal that eats its own kind.

Carnivore—an animal that eats meat.

Cocoon—a protective covering of silk produced by insect larvae to protect their bodies while they transform into adults.

Exoskeleton—a hard outer covering that protects and supports the bodies of many creepy crawlies.

Fang—a long sharp tooth; some fangs are designed to inject venom.

Gland—a part of an animal's body that is used to make particular substances, such as silk.

Insect—a kind of creepy crawly that has six legs; most insects also have wings.

Jaws—hinged structures around the mouth that allow some animals to bite and chew.

Larvae—grublike creatures that are the juvenile (young) stage in the life cycle of many insects.

Lizard—one of a group of mainly small-to medium-sized reptiles.

Mammal—one of a group of warm-blooded animals that have an internal skeleton and that feed their young on milk.

Molting—the shedding of a spider's exoskeleton; they have to shed their skin to grow.

Pedipalps—short, leglike organs that a spider uses to hold its food.

Predator—an animal that hunts and eats other animals.

Prey—an animal that is eaten by other animals.

Prosoma—the front part of a spider's body that consists of the head and the thorax fused together into a single body part.

Retractable—Something that can be taken in or drawn back.

Scorpion—a type of creature related to spiders; it has a long, flexible tail equipped with a venomous sting.

Silk—a natural thread produced by insect larvae and adult spiders.

Skeleton—an internal structure of bones that supports the bodies of large animals such as mammals, reptiles, and fish.

Spiderling—a young spider that is not yet fully grown.

Spinnerets—tiny nozzles on a spider's abdomen that are used to squirt out silk.

Tadpole—the juvenile (young) form of a frog or toad.

Terrarium—a container where plants and animals can live.

Thorax—the middle part of an insect's body where the legs are attached.

Venom—a poison produced by an animal for use against other animals.

Web—network of silk threads produced by many spiders to catch flying insects.

Index

A
abdomen 6–7, 13, 30
adults
    exoskeleton 5
    life cycle 28
    silk production 9
antilles pink toe 11
arachnids 5, 30
    see also spiders
arachnophobia 29, 30
arthropods 5, 30
    see also spiders

B
baby insects 9, 30
bird-eating tarantulas 4, 12–13, 19, 22, 29
bites 22–23, 25, 29
black widow spiders 25
Brazilian tarantulas 7, 19
burrows 9, 10, 20
    see also nests

C
cannibals 29, 30
carnivores 4, 11, 30
Chile rose tarantula 17
claws 29, 31
cocoons 9, 30
communication 18–19
crab spider 17
curved spiny spider 25

E
egg sac 20–21, 28
European wolf spider 22–3
exoskeleton 5, 21, 30
eyes 6, 14–15, 24

F
fangs 6, 10–11, 16–17, 30
females 8, 18–21, 28–29
flower spiders 25
food 17
    see also prey

G
glands 11, 30
goliath bird-eating tarantula 13

H
hairs 15, 23
head 6–7
humans 22–23, 25, 29

I
insects
    prey 4, 10–11, 13, 17
    shape 7
    silk production 9
    understanding 4–5, 30

J
jaws 6, 9, 11, 16–17, 22, 30
jumping spiders 15, 19, 24

L
larvae 9, 30
legs 6, 14–15, 19, 29
life cycle 28–29
liquefied food 17
liquid silk 13
lizards 13, 29, 30

M
males 8, 18–19, 29
mammals 13, 30
mating 18–19
metallic pink-toe tarantula 9
Mexican tarantulas 6–7, 14–15
molting 21, 29, 30

N
nests 8–9, 11
    see also burrows
net-throwing spiders 27

P
Pampas gold tarantula 19
Panama 8
pedipalps 6, 31
pet tarantulas 21, 29
pink tarantula 7
poison 23
    see also venom
predators 4, 12, 29, 31
prey 12–13, 31
    birds 4, 12–13, 19, 22, 29
    insects 4, 10–11, 13, 17
    liquefied 17
    mating partner 19
    silk 9
    trip lines 10–11
prosoma 6–7, 15–16, 31

R
raft spider 10
red-kneed tarantula 4, 7, 15
retractable claws 29, 31
rose tarantula 17

S
safety sounds 19
salmon bird-eating tarantula 19
scorpions 5, 31
senses 14–15
silk 31
    egg sac 20
    liquid 13
    production 7, 9
    spider behavior 26–27
skeleton 5, 31
snakes 13
sounds 19, 29
South America 5–8, 11, 13–15, 17
spider-eating predators 12, 29
spiderlings 20–1, 28–29, 31
spiders
    behavior 26–27
    development 21
    liquefied food 17
    senses 14–15
    shape 7
    silk production 9
    sounds 19
    types 24–5
    understanding 4–5
spinnerets 13, 31
spinning webs 10, 26–7
spiny spiders 25
spitting spider 27

T
tadpoles 27, 31
terrarium 29, 31
thorax 7, 31
tree homes 8
trip lines 9–11, 18

U
underground homes 8

V
venom 11, 22–23, 25, 31
vibrations 14–15

W
water spider 27
web spinners 26
webs 9–11, 26–27, 31
wolf spider 20–23